Teach Me

Penguin Learns the Skill of Self-Discipline

Illustrated by
Adam Riong

Written by
Charlotte Dane

THIS BOOK BELONGS TO

Penguin had such *amazing* habits.

His friends were all so impressed, and his parents and teachers never had to scold him.

If Penguin had math homework to finish, he would simply smile and say

"Work hard, play hard!
If I finish my math homework first, I can relax without a worry in the world and play video games!"

If Penguin had to walk the dog early in the morning, he would just tell himself

Getting an early start on the day is amazing!
So much more can be accomplished.

When Penguin had to clean his room every Sunday morning, he would think to himself

"Easy! It doesn't take long and it's better to do things little by little, instead of having them pile up at the end."

And when Penguin knew he had to practice the violin each day, he would shrug his shoulders and proclaim

"I'm so lucky to be able to work towards my goal of being an amazing violinist!"

Indeed, Penguin had amazing habits and willpower and self-discipline. But he was not always like this. In fact, he used to be the opposite and always ran away from all of his chores and duties!

F

Once upon a time, Penguin used to be quite impatient and careless. Penguin would hide his violin music.

He wouldn't clean his room for months.
He would do his homework at the last moment.
He would wait hours to walk his dog!

And worst of all, Penguin was frustrated, had a temper, and wasn't sure how to change things for the better!

Until one day, Fox, a friend of Penguin's, came to visit him after school to work together on a school project about dinosaurs.

Fox suggested a fun and easy way to change his thinking. "Do you want to know how I am never worried, and get things done so quickly and easily?"

"I used something called the 2-minute rule. You can count to 2 minutes, right? I know you can, no problem!"
2-MINUTE RULE

"All you need to do is do the task for
2 minutes!
That's it. That's your goal, and ignore
everything else."
?
11
10
9
8
7
6

"It couldn't be easier than that!
We can do almost anything for
2 minutes, right?
And it's sooo easy."

"But when you do something for 2 minutes, something magical happens. You get momentum."

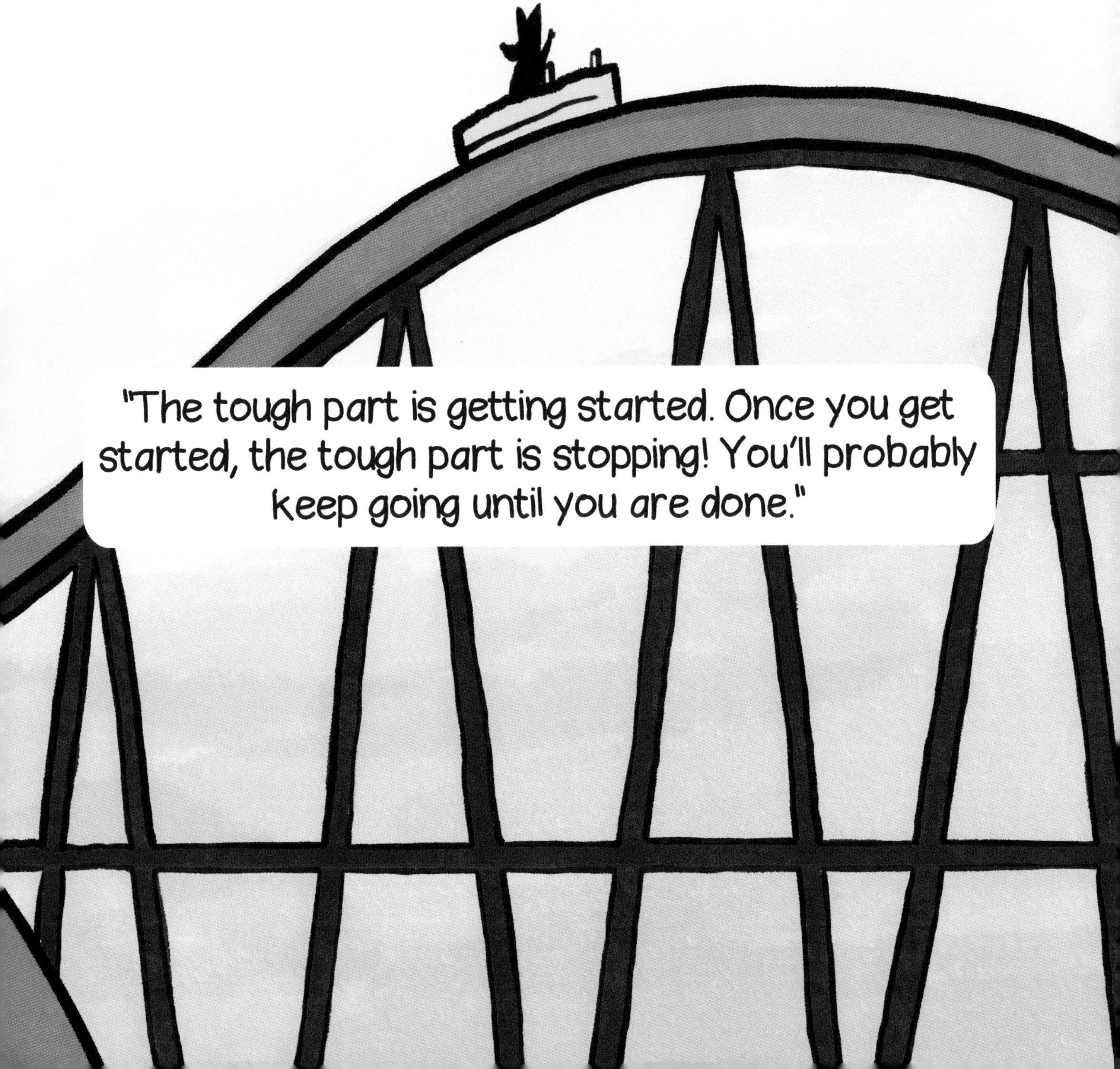
"The tough part is getting started. Once you get started, the tough part is stopping! You'll probably keep going until you are done."

At first, Penguin didn't believe it. Everything he didn't like to do felt like huge boulders he had to push uphill!

But he trusted and believed Fox, so the next morning when he had to walk the dog, he told himself, "Just 2 minutes! No problem!"

So he started counting. 1... 2...3...4...5...

And do you know what happened?

It worked! Penguin stopped counting after 47 seconds, and he ended up walking the dog for 20 minutes.

It wasn't hard at all, and the most difficult part was getting started.
Penguin felt like he had found a secret code!

The next day, Penguin had to do the same with cleaning his room. Just like the day before, he starting counting. 1...2...3...4..5...

And just like the day before, it worked like a charm.

From that day on, whenever Penguin had something he didn't want to do, he just started counting to 120 seconds, because he knew the hard part was just getting started. And he never had a problem with his willpower and self-discipline again.

The 2-minute rule just might be your secret weapon to achieving your goals and getting what you want!

Printed by Amazon Italia Logistica S.r.l.
Torrazza Piemonte (TO), Italy

21136686R00022